PENUMBRA™

d20 system

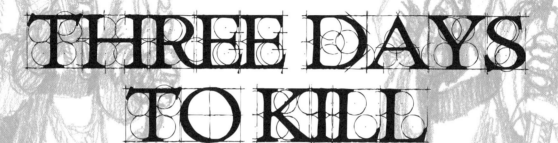

THREE DAYS TO KILL

AN ADVENTURE MODULE
FOR CHARACTERS
OF 1ST – 3RD LEVEL

Requires the use of the
Dungeons & Dragons® *Player's*
Handbook, Third Edition, pub-
lished by Wizards of the Coast®

BY JOHN TYNES

THREE DAYS TO KILL

CREDITS

AUTHOR: John Tynes
EDITOR: Michelle A. Brown Nephew
PUBLISHER & EDITORIAL ASSISTANCE: John Nephew
COVER GRAPHIC DESIGNER: John Tynes
COVER ILLUSTRATION: Richard Pace
INTERIOR GRAPHIC DESIGNER: Scott Reeves
INTERIOR ILLUSTRATIONS: Toren Atkinson, Scott Reeves, David White
CARTOGRAPHY AND FLOORPLANS: Michelle A. Brown Nephew, using
    Campaign Cartographer 2 from Profantasy Software. All maps contained in
    this book are available for download from the Atlas Games web site.
PUBLISHER'S SPECIAL THANKS: Jonathan Tweet, Rob Heinsoo, Ryan
    Dancey, and the editor who published my first D&D article in DRAGON
    Magazine 14 years ago: Kim Mohan
AUTHOR'S DEDICATION: To Jonathan Tweet, for building all those sandboxes

Dungeons & Dragons® and Wizards of the Coast® are Registered Trademarks of Wizards of the Coast, and are used with permission. This adventure module contains material based on the D20 System. The D20 System and D20 System logo are trademarks owned by Wizards of the Coast, and are used under the terms of the D20 Trademark License.

Penumbra is the trademark of Trident, Inc., d/b/a Atlas Games for its line of D20 fantasy roleplaying game supplements. Atlas Games and "Charting New Realms of Imagination" are trademarks of John Nephew, used under license. The Atlas Games logo is a trademark of John Nephew and Trident, Inc., d/b/a Atlas Games.

Copyright ©2000 John Tynes. Published under license by Trident, Inc., d/b/a Atlas Games.

This is a work of fiction. Any resemblance to actual events or persons, living or dead, is purely coincidental.

The following text is ©1999 Wizards of the Coast. All Rights Reserved. Used with permission. No permission is granted to reprint or redistribute this text in any media without the prior written consent of the Copyright Holder. To request such permission, please contact ryand@frpg.com (Ryan Dancey).

D20 SYSTEM TRADEMARK LICENSE
Version 0.4
1. Definitions.
1.1. "License" means this document.
1.2. "Publication" means any distribution of material under the terms of this License.
1.3. "D20 System Trademarks" means the words "D20 System", and the D20 System logo.
1.4. "D20 System Reference Document" means the copyrighted work owned by Wizards of the Coast identified by that name.
1.5. Each licensee is addressed as "You".
2. The License.
2.1 Offer and Acceptance: Wizards of the Coast offers You the right to Accept the terms of this License. You are permitted to use the D20 System Trademarks only in compliance with this License. Use of the Trademarks under any other circumstances is permissible only with explicit written permission from Wizards of the Coast. Distribution of any Publication which uses the D20 System Trademarks indicates your acceptance of the terms of this License.
2.2 Consideration: In consideration for agreeing to use this License, Wizards of the Coast hereby grants You a world-wide, royalty-free, non-exclusive license to use the D20 System Trademarks as described in this License.
3. Terms and Conditions.
3.1 Limitation of License
3.1.1. No Publication distributed under the terms of this License may contain information on creating characters compatible with the D20 System Reference Document v0.0.
3.1.2. No Publication distributed under the terms of this License may contain information explaining the effects on characters of earning experience or advancing in "level" as that term is defined in the D20 System Reference Document v0.0.
3.1.3. The document known as the D20 System Reference Document v0.0 contains a section titled

"Restricted Terms and Definitions". You may not use any term described in that section in any way other than as described in that section in a Publication covered by this License. If the D20 System Reference Document is revised by Wizards of the Coast, you may use any version of the "Restricted Terms and Definitions" section of any version of the D20 System Reference Document issued by Wizards of the Coast.
3.2. Required Notices
3.2.1. You must include a copy of this License with every Publication covered by this License that you distribute.
3.3. Wizards of the Coast Logos and Trademarks.
3.3.1. You may place a notice in the Publication that reads: "Requires the use of the Dungeons & Dragons(R) Player's Handbook, Third Edition, published by Wizards of the Coast(R)." If typography permits, the "(R)" indicia should be converted to the recognized "circle R" character.
3.3.2. If you use the provisions in 3.3.1. you must attach the following notice to the Publication: "Dungeons & Dragons(R) and Wizards of the Coast(R) are Registered Trademarks of Wizards of the Coast, and are used with Permission." If typography permits, the "(R)" indicia should be converted to the recognized "circle R" character.
3.3.3. You may not use the Dungeons & Dragons(R) or Wizards of the Coast(R) trademarks in advertising or in any material separate from the Publication, or in any other way other than that described in Section 3.3.1 and 3.3.2.
3.4. Use of the D20 System Logo
3.4.1. If the Publication is not an electronic file, You must include on the either the front, spine, or back cover of a Publication distributed under the terms of this License the graphical icon known as the "D20 System" logo, which must appear at a size no smaller than .5 (one half) inches by .5 (one half) inches.
3.4.2. If the Publication is an electronic file, the "d20 System" logo must appear in the first area of the Publication displayed when a user views the Publication under normal conditions. The logo must not be smaller than .5 (one half) inches by .5 (one half) inches.
3.4.3. If an Electronic Publication cannot reproduce a graphic element (for example, an ASCII text file),

the file must contain the text "This file contains material based on the D20 System. The D20 System and the D20 System logo are trademarks owned by Wizards of the Coast and used under the terms of the D20 Trademark License."
3.4.4. The logo may not be obscured by any other graphic element.
3.4.5. No other alterations of the "D20 System" logo are permissible.
3.5. Permission to use the D20 System Trademarks
3.5.1. You are granted permission to use the "D20 System" Trademarks in advertising connected with a Publication distributed under the terms of this License.
3.5.2. You are granted permission to use the D20 System Trademarks in advertising copy and package copy to describe any Publication distributed under the terms of this License.
3.5.3. You are prohibited from claiming ownership or Trademark interest in the "D20 System" logo, or the "D20 System" trademarks.
3.5.4. You are prohibited from using the "D20 System" logo or the "D20 System" Trademarks in association with a Publication that does not include content derived at least in part from the D20 System Reference Document.
4. Inability to Comply Due to Statute or Regulation. If it is impossible for You to comply with any of the terms of this License with respect to some or all of the Covered Materials due to statute, judicial order, or governmental regulation then You may not Publish any Covered Material so affected.
6. Termination.
This License and the rights granted hereunder will terminate automatically if You fail to comply with all terms herein and fail to cure such breach within 30 days of becoming aware of the breach. All sublicenses to the Covered Materials which are properly granted shall survive any termination of this License. Provisions which, by their nature, must remain in effect beyond the termination of this License shall survive.
7. Miscellaneous.
If any provision of this License is held to be unenforceable, such provision shall be reformed only to the extent necessary to make it enforceable.

ATLAS GAMES

PO BOX 131233 • ROSEVILLE, MN 55113
INFO@ATLAS-GAMES.COM • WWW.ATLAS-GAMES.COM

SECOND PRINTING • SEPTEMBER 2000
ISBN 1-887801-94-4

THREE DAYS TO KILL

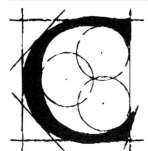

CONTENTS

CHAPTER ONE

BACKDROP

With some jobs, you can hire just any dumb group of joes. Guarding a caravan? Kidnapped princess? Rogue minotaur? No problem — just send your resident creepy old guy in a cloak down to the local tavern and hire the first group of dullards in shiny new armor you can find. Jobs like that are a dime a dozen, and pay about as much.

Other jobs … well, other jobs can be different. Sometimes you need some people to do some work that might not strike the village idiot as exactly on the up-and-up. There's danger involved, sure, and maybe at the end of the day your band of for-hire thugs can convince themselves that they did something worthwhile. But the job isn't about doing something worthwhile. It's about putting the hurt on someone for the sake of your interests. It's about doing a number on the competition. It's about greed — your greed, your victim's greed, and of course the greed of your hired thugs.

Jobs like that aren't easy to come by. They sure aren't easy to pull off.

But man, they really pay well …

Three Days To Kill is a scenario for a group of low-level characters. The storyline is very straightforward, offering opportunities for exploration, surveillance, infiltration, and combat. The only way players can really screw things up is if they die trying. The toughest part of running this scenario is adjusting the enemy forces to best match the group, and even this isn't too tough; options exist to introduce additional foes in the midst of combat if the initial group of bad guys isn't enough.

Our story is set in a small area known as the Deeps, a valley surrounded by mountains that lies along a major east-west trade route. The heart of the Deeps is Deeptown, a major waypoint for caravans, which practices a policy of openness to anyone willing to spend a little money — or, preferably, a lot.

The player characters are hired by a local bandit lord to make a hit on a rival. This rival is holding a secret meeting with some potential allies at a villa in the mountains, and the PCs' new employer wants them to disrupt the meeting. They don't have to kill everybody, so long as they ruin the event and demonstrate to the potential allies what a loser the rival is. The bandit lord wants to break up this new partnership before it gets off the ground.

The potential allies in question are members of a religious group called the Sect of Sixty, diabolical priests who traffick with devils. Throw in some snooping clerics from a holy order, a few young orcs out to prove their manhood, and a surprise straight from Hell. Stir briskly and bring to a boil.

Things are about to get *hot*.

4

CUSTOMIZATION

This scenario is designed to be adapted into most any fantasy campaign. Although the geography of the locale and the politics of the area are very specific and very important to the scenario, they are still pretty well self-contained and transportable. In particular, the deities worshipped by the various temples of Deeptown are never named; you should choose appropriate gods from your campaign world to fill those slots. If instead you simply want to run this scenario as a one-off without any particular fantasy world attached, you should find everything you need in these pages.

In several places, more information is given than you need for this scenario. The author's intention here is to provide you with source material for further adventures in the Deeps, and several suggestions along these lines appear at the end of the book.

SETTING

The Deeps is the name of a valley within a mountain range, called the Deeps because the mountains frequently put the valley in shadow. In the heart of the valley is Deeptown, a waypoint on the east-west trade route that passes through the mountains. Deeptown is located on the shores of Shadow Lake, a largish body of water fed by two rivers, Forks and Dream, coming down from the mountains to the north.

The mountainous terrain of the trade route makes caravans easy pickings for bandits, leading to a steady job market in low-brain, high-brawn caravan guardsmanship. The towns on either side of the mountains are about three days' journey either way, making Deeptown a destination point for young toughs looking for work — pay rates for caravans leaving Deeptown are often double those of the outside towns, since if you're hiring in Deeptown it means you've already been hit on one side of the mountains and now need reinforcements to get through the other. Despite a steady stream of fresh guards, the job market remains tight; casualties are high, and the more-capable guards sometimes join the local bandit lords for even better pay.

There are six bandit lords in the area. Calling them "lords" gives them too much credit, really — they're just competent thugs. The largest two groups — those controlled by the bandits Modus and Lucien — each have about two dozen men, while the smallest are no more than a half-dozen leaden scum out for quick profits. The smaller groups stage frequent hit-and-run attacks, often just stealing horses and whatever coin wealthy-looking travelers happen to have on their persons. The two large groups attack fewer caravans, and they tend to make well-executed assaults that strip their targets clean. None of the groups are especially bloodthirsty; they usually tangle with the guards, killing some, but leave the merchants and travelers alive when all is said and done. If they just slaughtered everyone who came through this wouldn't be a trade route for long, so the leadership of Deeptown wouldn't tolerate that sort of extreme behavior. When the occasional group of psychos turns up and murders every traveler in

ILLUSTRATION BY TOREN ATKINSON

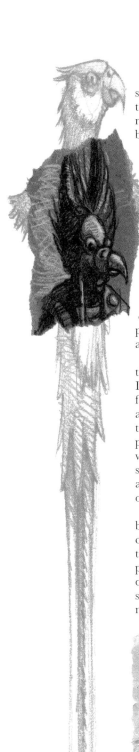

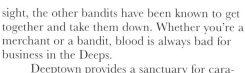

sight, the other bandits have been known to get together and take them down. Whether you're a merchant or a bandit, blood is always bad for business in the Deeps.

Deeptown provides a sanctuary for caravans, and of course engages in a form of fleecing of its own. Prices for most goods and services are high, since there's no competition, but Deeptown's status as a major waypoint ensures that it has both a wide variety and a good quality of merchandise. It's one of the few towns in the region where you can commonly purchase exotic spices, fabrics, and even magic items. After all, what the caravans don't sell to the merchants of Deeptown, the bandits do. Entertainment is also common, with festhalls, minstrels, festivals, and passion plays, all of which separate merchants and travelers from their money.

On the higher side of life, Deeptown is home to the outposts of numerous religious groups. Dozens of small temples welcome travelers of all faiths who are looking for a little reassurance about their prospects on the mountain road. The town's welcome-to-all mentality means that temples dedicated to both good and evil can be found within, to the frequent chagrin and occasional shouting matches of the faithful. Some temples also provide banking services, a valuable source of income to the faithful.

The town is governed by a council entirely beholden to the interests of commerce. The council levies slight taxes on the ample trade industry to fund the town guard, which prosecutes and punishes criminal activity as well as providing for defense and public safety. Most public services, such as road repair, are paid for by self-appointed neighborhood associations that double as legit-

imized protection rackets, pressuring residents and businesspeople in the neighborhood to cough up money to pay for such services.

Contract disputes and violations of civil law are adjudicated by the Trade Circle, a self-appointed group of the seven most prosperous businesspeople in town. Privately, the Trade Circle is the true power in Deeptown; the town council would never act against their wishes.

It's hard to really call this system corrupt — it's so nakedly self-serving that there's no real deception involved. In Deeptown, you get exactly what you're willing to pay for.

DEEPTOWN ORGANIZATION

As shown in the center spread map, Deeptown is an octagonal walled enclave about two miles in diameter. The walls are earthen mounds, not worked stone, and rise sharply to a height of about twenty feet. The angle is not so steep that you can't walk up the side, but it's steep enough that you can't do so very quickly. The perimeter includes thirteen wooden towers that rise a further fifteen feet above the wall, each set at a 45 degree angle to the wall so that there are two walls facing the exterior. Each tower is twelve feet square and has two doors on the rear walls with sturdy bars on the inside for defense. The ground floor contains four cross-shaped arrow slits on each of the two exterior walls. A steep wooden staircase inside runs up to an open platform that forms the roof, with wooden battlements five feet tall that contain additional arrow slits identical to those of the

Rumors

At your discretion, the PCs may hear various rumors around Deeptown. These have nothing to do with this scenario, but could be expanded into further, unrelated adventures.

- They don't call it the Dream River for nothing. The mouth of the river is said to issue from atop a lonely mountain somewhere to the north. Traveling upriver into the heart of the mountain, the curious may find an abandoned, underground temple where the dreams of mortals take physical form. On certain nights of the year, the water of the river is said to possess magic powers — if you drink from it close to the source, at least.

- When the Trade Circle chased out the House of Good Favor last year (see page 21), the priest left behind a treasure cache composed of money defrauded from credulous citizens. Although the building is abandoned and well-looted, rumors persist of a secret room beneath the ground where the priest hid his ill-gotten gains. It is said to be guarded by a magical protector.

- There is an insane giant living in the southern mountains, driven mad by a vengeful wizard. Although he is ferocious, he is said to have a sizable hoard of treasure.

- Occasionally, rafts manned by strange, silent elves come down the Forks River to Shadow Lake. They drift into the lake by night and are never seen again.

- Bonfires are sometimes seen on a mountain to the west. According to legend, a temple of female priests reside there, murdering any man who glimpses their secret orgiastic rituals — but they're awfully tempting to watch.

ground floor. The roof platform also contains a hand-pulled bell to sound the alarm.

The wall is broken in three places by wooden gatehouses, in the center of the east, west, and south walls. These gatehouses each contain an iron portcullis controlled from the roof platform, which also permits uninterrupted travel along the top of the wall. The gates are left open from sunrise to sunset. They may be opened for travelers arriving by night with the approval of the city guard commander at each gate. The gates are

named for the bodies of water nearest them; the west gate is called Forks Gate, the east is Dream Gate, and the south is Lake Gate, named for Shadow Lake which lies two hundred yards south of town.

Each of the wall structures, including towers and gates, are staffed by six guards at all times. By night, an additional dozen guards walk the wall in a steady rotation.

Attacks against Deeptown are rare. In the last fifty years, there has only been one

Modus

Fearless Leader, 5th-Level Fighter

Hit Dice:	5d10+10 (42 hp)
Initiative:	+6 (+2 Dex, +4 Improved Initiative)
Speed:	20 ft.
AC:	19 (+5 Breastplate, +2 Dex, +2 Large Shield)
Attacks:	Longsword +9 melee
Damage:	Longsword 1d8+5
Face/Reach:	5 ft. by 5 ft./5 ft.
Saves:	Fort +6, Ref +3, Will +3
Abilities:	Str 17, Dex 15, Con 15, Int 14, Wis 12, Cha 14
Skills:	Appraise +8, Bluff +4, Hide -2 (incl. -6 armor penalty), Listen +3, Ride +9, Spot +3, Wilderness Lore +2
Feats:	Improved Initiative, Quick Draw, Mounted Combat, Weapon Focus (Longsword), Weapon Specialization (Longsword)
Challenge Rating:	5
Alignment:	Neutral

Ring of Protection from Spells: Grants the wearer a constant +8 modifier to all saving throws versus spells.

Lucien

Ambitious Bandit, 4th-Level Fighter

Hit Dice:	4d10+8 (28 hp)
Initiative:	+6 (+2 Dex, +4 Improved Initiative)
Speed:	20 ft.
AC:	19 (+5 Chainmail, +2 Dex, +2 Large Shield)
Attacks:	Longsword +9 melee
Damage:	Longsword 1d8+5
Face/Reach:	5 ft. by 5 ft./5 ft.
Saves:	Fort +6, Ref +3, Will +1
Abilities:	Str 16, Dex 14, Con 14, Int 13, Wis 10, Cha 13
Skills:	Climb +1 (incl. -7 armor penalty), Diplomacy +5, Hide +4, Jump -2 (incl. -7 armor penalty), Listen +1, Spot +2
Feats:	Improved Initiative, Mounted Combat, Ride-By Attack, Weapon Focus (Longsword), Weapon Specialization (Longsword)
Challenge Rating:	4
Alignment:	Neutral

serious assault by a traveling and rather stupid orc tribe consisting of about forty warriors. They were repelled handily, thanks in particular to the temple clerics of the town who assisted in the defense. Some of the more prosperous merchants also have wizards on retainer to help when needed.

Within the walls, Deeptown is generally laid out on a very strict grid system of streets. This system was imposed by the original Trade Circle two hundred years ago, and was built around the core of Old Town, the first settlement on this trade route. Today, Old Town retains its quaint and rather random layout of streets and plazas, surrounded by the far more orderly neighborhoods that reach to the walls. There are four neighborhoods outside Old Town. The western ones are Upper Forks and Lower Forks, while the eastern are Upper Dream and Lower Dream. There are unofficial names for many of the subsections of these neighborhoods as well.

Each grid block outside Old Town is about two hundred yards square and is bordered by streets on all sides. Within each block, however, there are usually a number of alleys, courtyards, and even minor roads that have grown up within the structure imposed by the Trade Circle.

The Town Council, official seat of governance, is located in Deeptown Hall within Old Town. All bureaucratic aspects of Deeptown are maintained therein except for the Town Guard and Jail, located a few streets away, where criminal activity is prosecuted and punished. The Trade Circle, which governs mostly behind the scenes, has no fixed location. The members typically meet either in one of their private residences or in a back room at one of Deeptown's finer inns. On those occasions when the group must adjudicate some public situation, such as a contractual dispute, the hearings are held at Deeptown Hall.

Deeptown has the usual level of crime found in any large settlement, but it is concentrated more in misbehavior than organized theft. For example, there is no guild of thieves; all attempts at consolidating that much criminal power have been ruthlessly crushed by the Trade Circle. Instead, crime in Deeptown revolves around bar brawls, independent cutpurses, and private disputes.

Of course, some would describe the highly organized system of patronage and taxation practiced by the Trade Circle as criminal behavior. But they wouldn't do so in public.

The Circle's crackdown on organized criminality within Deeptown ends at the earthen walls, and the town guard has never been dispatched in pursuit of the bandits who prey on caravans traveling through the Deeps. To an extent, the Circle considers bandit activity to be good for business, since it increases the value of Deeptown's security and services. No bandits have become enough of a

Maxlus

2nd-Level Fighter

Hit Dice:	2d10+2 (19 hp)
Initiative:	+5 (+2 Dex, +4 Improved Initiative)
Speed:	20 ft.
AC:	17 (+4 Scale Mail, +1 Dex, +2 Large Shield)
Attacks:	Longsword +5 melee, or Dagger +4 melee
Damage:	Longsword 1d8+2, Dagger 1d4+2
Face/Reach:	5 ft. by 5 ft./5 ft.
Saves:	Fort +4, Ref +1, Will +0
Abilities:	Str 15, Dex 12, Con 12, Int 11, Wis 11, Cha 12
Skills:	Climb +0 (incl. -6 armor penalty), Handle Animal +2, Jump -2 (incl. -6 armor penalty), Ride +2, Swim +4
Feats:	Endurance, Improved Initiative, Mounted Combat, Weapon Focus (Longsword)
Challenge Rating:	2
Alignment:	Neutral

Typical Maxlus Fighter

1st-Level Fighter

Hit Dice:	1d10+1 (10 hp)
Initiative:	+4 (Improved Initiative)
Speed:	20 ft.
AC:	15 (+3 Studded Leather, +2 Large Shield)
Attacks:	Longsword +3 melee, or Dagger +2 melee
Damage:	Longsword 1d8+1, Dagger 1d4+1
Face/Reach:	5 ft. by 5 ft./5 ft.
Saves:	Fort +3, Ref +0, Will +0
Abilities:	Str 13, Dex 10, Con 12, Int 10, Wis 10, Cha 10
Skills:	Climb -2 (incl. -3 armor penalty), Handle Animal +1, Jump -1 (incl. -3 armor penalty), Ride +3, Spot +1, Wilderness Lore +1
Feats:	Improved Initiative, Mounted Combat, Weapon Focus (Longsword)
Challenge Rating:	1
Alignment:	Neutral

threat to jeopardize use of the trade route through the Deeps, since groups who grow too large tend to attack each other. On a few occasions, the Trade Circle has hired private groups of adventurers to punish bandits who grew too dangerous. This has exerted evolutionary pressure on the region's bandits, resulting in the propagation of groups who are careful to neither shed too much blood in the course of their work nor assault too many travelers. As with most people in the Deeps, the Trade Circle prefers the invisible hand of the marketplace over the authoritarian rule of government; the paradox that it nevertheless exerts an authoritarian, though invisible, hand on the marketplace does not trouble its members in the slightest.

THE BANDIT LORDS

Modus and Lucien are the two toughest bandit lords in the area. They each got their start leading small raiding parties about six years ago, but their intelligence and charisma ensured that their respective groups prospered while others withered or fled. Two years ago they met and divided the territory around Deeptown between them: Modus took the west and Lucien took the east. While they have a nonaggression pact, they consider any other bandits in the area fair game.

The pair are unusually forward-thinking. At the time of their pact, they could both see a point when their strength would be too great for the Trade Circle of Deeptown to ignore — a point at which they could move into protection rackets, where caravans who paid for expensive Trade Circle permits would be spared in favor of those who didn't pay up. At some point, they agreed, they would be pretty much out of the bandit business and would instead become part of the Deeptown establishment.

Anticipating this, their pact includes the provision that neither will make an alliance with the leadership of Deeptown unless both are part of it. They rightly figure that they can strike a better bargain if they present a unified front.

Thus far, however, that day has not come. The Trade Circle still considers the bandit lords to be rabble scum, and is not interested in any bargains.

But Lucien is getting impatient. He resents both Modus's power and the haughty disdain of the Trade Circle. So he's hatched a plan that,

Antigen

2nd-Level Fighter

Hit Dice:	2d10 (16 hp)
Initiative:	+6 (+2 Dex, +4 Improved Initiative)
Speed:	20 ft.
AC:	16 (+4 Scale Mail, +2 Dex)
Attacks:	Longbow +5 ranged, or Shortsword +3 melee
Damage:	Longbow 1d8, Shortsword 1d6+1
Face/Reach:	5 ft. by 5 ft./5 ft.
Saves:	Fort +2, Ref +2, Will +0
Abilities:	Str 12, Dex 15, Con 11, Int 12, Wis 10, Cha 11
Skills:	Climb -1 (incl. -4 armor penalty), Craft (Bowmaking) +7, Handle Animal +2, Jump -1 (incl. -4 armor penalty), Ride +5, Swim +3
Feats:	Improved Initiative, Mounted Archery, Mounted Combat, Weapon Focus (Longbow)
Challenge Rating:	2
Alignment:	Neutral

Typical Antigen Archer

1st-Level Fighter

Hit Dice:	1d10+1 (10 hp)
Initiative:	+4 (Improved Initiative)
Speed:	20 ft.
AC:	14 (+4 Scale Mail)
Attacks:	Longbow +5 ranged, or Shortsword +2 melee
Damage:	Longbow 1d8, Shortsword 1d6+1
Face/Reach:	5 ft. by 5 ft./5 ft.
Saves:	Fort +3, Ref +2, Will +0
Abilities:	Str 12, Dex 14, Con 12, Int 10, Wis 10, Cha 10
Skills:	Climb -3 (incl. -4 armor penalty), Handle Animal +1, Jump -3 (incl. -4 armor penalty), Ride +5, Spot +1, Wilderness Lore +1
Feats:	Improved Initiative, Mounted Combat, Weapon Focus (Longbow)
Challenge Rating:	1
Alignment:	Neutral

while not technically violating the pact, still gives him the edge he needs to crush Modus, consolidate power, and then make his move on the Deeptown establishment. Lucien has offered a secret alliance to the diabolical Sect of Sixty, which maintains a temple in Deeptown and would like nothing better than to gain bureaucratic and taxation power over this lucrative trade route — covertly, of course. Lucien's proposed alliance would have the Sect providing supernatural aid to crush Modus, and then acting as a silent partner to Lucien as he consolidates his power over the valley and makes an offer to the Trade Circle that they can't refuse. From the Sect's perspective, it's perfect: it can't make such a blatant power grab openly for fear of sparking a religious war with the Holy Order, but with Lucien as its catspaw, the Sect can gain power and wealth indirectly. Of course, both Lucien and the Sect are confident that the other can be easily controlled.

Modus has gotten wind of Lucien's plan, although he does not know that the Sect is the potential ally. He believes that Lucien is making a deal with someone on the Trade Circle.

At the same time, the head of the local Holy Order temple, Cassius, has heard rumors from the opposite end: the Sect is meeting with a powerful ally who will help it gain control of the valley. But he has no idea that the ally is Lucien; his best guess is that it's the orcs of the Hard Tribe who live beyond the mountains to the north.

What both Modus and Cassius do know is that their respective opponents are meeting with the secretive new ally at an abandoned villa in the mountains to discuss the deal. Cassius has dispatched two acolytes to investigate and report back. Modus is taking the direct approach: he's hiring a group of freelance adventurers to make a raid on the villa and hopefully squash the deal.

Even if the raid goes poorly, he can claim that the attackers were just another small bandit group with no connections to his organization, or that they were even hired by the Trade Circle or the Holy Order. With so many factions vying for power, there's plenty of blame to go around.

MODUS'S RAIDERS

Modus has a group of twenty bandits, divided into two teams of nine troops each led by a lieutenant. The two lieutenants, Maxlus and Antigen, specialize in close-in fighting and sniper support, respectively.

LUCIEN'S CIRCLE

Lucien's group numbers twenty-three, separated into two squads of nine and one squad of five. He has no lieutenants, as he does not trust anyone else to lead his troops. The two larger squads are both assault groups, while the smaller and more skilled team stays with Lucien as a free squad to fight where needed.

Typical Assault Squad Fighter

0-Level Fighter

Hit Dice:	1d10 (4 hp)
Initiative:	+0
Speed:	20 ft.
AC:	12 (+2 Leather)
Attacks:	Longsword +1 melee
Damage:	Longsword 1d8
Face/Reach:	5 ft. by 5 ft./5 ft.
Saves:	Fort +2, Ref +0, Will +0
Abilities:	Str 11, Dex 10, Con 11, Int 10, Wis 10, Cha 10
Skills:	Ride +1, Spot +1
Feats:	Weapon Focus (Longsword)
Challenge Rating:	1/2
Alignment:	Neutral

Typical Free Squad Fighter

1st-Level Fighter

Hit Dice:	1d10+1 (10 hp)
Initiative:	+4 (Improved Initiative)
Speed:	20 ft.
AC:	14 (+4 Scale Mail)
Attacks:	Longsword +3 melee, or Dagger +2 melee
Damage:	Longsword 1d8+1, Dagger 1d4+1
Face/Reach:	5 ft. by 5 ft./5 ft.
Saves:	Fort +3, Ref +0, Will +0
Abilities:	Str 12, Dex 11, Con 12, Int 10, Wis 10, Cha 10
Skills:	Climb -2 (incl. -4 armor penalty), Handle Animal +1, Jump -2 (incl. -4 armor penalty), Ride +3, Spot +1, Wilderness Lore +1
Feats:	Improved Initiative, Mounted Combat, Weapon Focus (Longsword)
Challenge Rating:	1
Alignment:	Neutral

THE DEEPTOWN TEMPLES

Deeptown's status as a major trade waypoint has ensured that the town as a whole serves no god but commerce itself. Various sects have made offers of protection in the past, in exchange for a sort of religious franchise that would see rival sects chased out of town; these have always been rejected. Deeptown's Trade Circle believes that the best thing for business is to welcome anyone and everyone, so long as the peace is kept and money can endlessly change hands.

As a result, Deeptown is home to numerous temples small and large, many of whom would be at each other's throats in other cities. Temples of manifest and diabolical evil are as welcome as those of resolute good, with the understanding that they are all here only to provide worship ser-

vices for the traveling faithful and to proselytize to anyone willing to listen. Twelve years ago a new priest of the Clench of Might arrived to lead the Deeptown temple and promptly launched a bloody assault on the Temple of the Free Spirit. A cabal of acolytes from thirteen other temples, directed by the Trade Circle, captured the Clench priest and he was executed on the Old Town Commons by the town guard; that night, the Clench of Might temple was ransacked by the cabal and burned to the ground. After six years of expensive negotiations with the Trade Circle, the Clench was eventually allowed to build a new temple and installed a more accommodating priest.

Instead of viewing Deeptown as an expansionist power base, the temples here see their mission as akin to advertising. The larger temples invest heavily in expensive buildings and

The Temple of the Holy Order

0 5 10 15 20 25 30

SCALE IN FEET

ornamentation, as well as hosting extravagant festivals to celebrate their beliefs and communicate their myths. But even the smaller ones provide important services to the traveling faithful, especially banking — a traveler can deposit money with his or her preferred temple in Deeptown and receive a letter of deposit redeemable at other allied temples nearby. Such letters are useless in the hands of anyone other than the depositor, making them a handy way to avoid carrying large quantities of money desirable to bandits. (Of course, the fees for such banking services are substantial, and many caravan leaders prefer to keep their assets liquid and intact.) Other services offered by the temples include food and lodging that conforms to the practices of the faith, as well as the usual worship opportunities. In addition, many of the temples offer a sort of caravan-guard accreditation. Prospective guards can submit to a battery of tests to establish their beliefs and trustworthiness, and are then offered to like-aligned caravans with a guarantee of moral reliability. (This accreditation typically costs prospective guards 5 gp, but grants +10 to initial Bargain skill checks with like-aligned caravan masters.)

Although there are thirty-eight temples in Deeptown, only two are important to this scenario: the Holy Order and the Sect of Sixty.

THE HOLY ORDER

The Holy Order is a religious sect devoted to the preservation of life. The Deeptown temple is led by the priest Cassius, who has been instructed by his masters to spread the glory of their beliefs. Owing to the peculiar status of Deeptown, he is forbidden from taking direct action against the forces of evil. Instead, he invests the temple's sizable donations in making the building ever-more beautiful and elaborate, as well as in putting on regular passion plays and festivals. Much of the temple's funding comes from banking revenues. The Order maintains closely allied temples in towns to the west and east of the valley, specifically to provide financial security from bandits to caravans passing through — but only, of course, to those caravan leaders willing to convert to the Order's stringent faith.

Although Cassius follows his orders well, he can't resist taking what actions he can against the forces of destruction. Specifically, he has developed an intelligence network of spies and informants that helps him keep tabs on rival temples, including the Sect of Sixty. Aside from religious rivals, Cassius is also worried about the Hard Tribe, a large group of orcs that lives in the

Cassius

8th-Level Cleric, A Disciplined Disciple

Hit Dice:	8d8+8 (61 hp)
Initiative:	+1 (Dex)
Speed:	20 ft.
AC:	17 (+6 Banded Mail, +1 Dex)
Attacks:	Longsword +8/+3 melee
Damage:	Longsword 1d8+2
Face/Reach:	5 ft. by 5 ft./5 ft.
Special Qualities:	Normal cleric powers
Saves:	Fort +1, Ref +3, Will +9
Abilities:	Str 14, Dex 12, Con 13, Int 16, Wis 17, Cha 14
Skills:	Diplomacy +9, Gather Information +6, Heal +9, Intimidate +6, Knowledge (Religion) +8, Ride +4, Scry +9, Sense Motive +6, Spellcraft +6
Feats	Extra Turning, Heighten Spell, Maximize Spell, Toughness
Challenge Rating:	8
Alignment:	Lawful Good

Spells: Cassius typically prepares the following spells. He also has the 1st- through 4th-level domain spells for Good and Law.

0 Level: *cure minor wounds, detect magic, detect poison, guidance, purify food and drink, read magic*
1st Level: *bless water, command, comprehend languages, detect evil, divine favor*
2nd Level: *animal messenger, augury, gentle repose, hold person*
3rd Level: *cure serious wounds x4*
4th Level: *dismissal, restoration*
Good Domain: *protection from evil, aid, magic circle against evil, holy smite*
Law Domain: *protection from chaos, calm emotions, magic circle against chaos, order's wrath*

foothills of the northernmost mountains. The orcs are primarily interested in the fertile plains that lie beyond the mountains, but occasionally make incursions south into the Deeps. The Trade Circle certainly has no great love for the orcs, but does not consider them much of a threat. Cassius, on the other hand, fears the possibility of an alliance between the orcs and one of the darker temples, and often sends acolytes into the mountains to watch for tribal activity.

A map of the Holy Order temple appears on page 11. The temple is shaped as an octagonal flower, with thick stone walls that rise forty feet. Inside are eight altars, each backed by a V-shaped paper screen. Penitents may gather at any altar for prayer and guidance by an attending acolyte. A spiral staircase in the center leads to a basement, containing living quarters for the priest and acolytes as well as a kitchen and other mundanities.

THE SECT OF SIXTY

The Sect of Sixty is a thinly spread religious group devoted to the adoration of the diabolic. Its name derives from the fact that the Sect permits no more than sixty temple priests at a time, ensuring a steady traffic in intrigue and assassination designed to weed out the weak in favor of the strong.

Owing to its small size but wide dispersal, the Sect has opted to avoid the standard evil-group approach of conquest by force; instead, it seeks to foster its ideals through the promotion of selfishness and indulgent pleasure, a form of eroded morality that puts the self above all and encourages the lust for power. It pursues this goal by operating temples that include festhalls and frequent orgies of pleasure, magic, and food, all of which come at ever-

Typical Order Acolyte

1st-Level Cleric

Hit Dice:	1d8 (8 hp)
Initiative:	+0
Speed:	20 ft.
AC:	12 (+2 Leather Armor)
Attacks:	Longsword +0 melee
Damage:	Longsword 1d8
Face/Reach:	5 ft. by 5 ft./5 ft.
Special Qualities:	Normal cleric powers
Saves:	Fort +2, Ref +0, Will +4
Abilities:	Str 10, Dex 11, Con 10, Int 13, Wis 14, Cha 11
Skills:	Concentration +2, Diplomacy +1, Heal +4, Knowledge (Religion) +3, Scry +2, Sense Motive +2, Spellcraft +3
Feats:	Extra Turning, Maximize Spell
Challenge Rating:	1
Alignment:	Lawful Good

Spells: A Holy Order acolyte typically prepares the following spells. He also has the 1st-level domain spells for Good and Law.
0 Level: *create water, detect magic, read magic*
1st Level: *command, cure light wounds*
Good Domain: *protection from evil*
Law Domain: *protection from chaos*

Typical Sect Acolyte

1st-Level Cleric

Hit Dice:	1d8 (8 hp)
Initiative:	+4 (Inproved Initiative)
Speed:	20 ft.
AC:	15 (+4 Chain Shirt, +1 Small Shield)
Attacks:	Longsword +0 melee
Damage:	Longsword 1d8
Face/Reach:	5 ft. by 5 ft./5 ft.
Special Qualities:	Normal cleric powers
Saves:	Fort +2, Ref +0, Will +4
Abilities:	Str 11, Dex 11, Con 10, Int 12, Wis 14, Cha 12
Skills:	Bluff +3, Diplomacy +3, Disguise +3, Hide -1 (incl. -3 armor penalty), Knowledge (Religion) +3, Spellcraft +3
Feats:	Improved Initiative, Maximize Spell
Challenge Rating:	1
Alignment:	Lawful Evil

Spells: A Sect of Sixty acolyte typically prepares the following spells. He also has the 1st-level domain spells for Evil and Trickery.
0 Level: *light, detect magic, resistance*
1st Level: *doom, inflict light wounds*
Evil Domain: *protection from good*
Trickery Domain: *change self*

escalating prices. The lower levels of activity simply require money, and are open to anyone with a taste for debauchery. Higher levels are restricted to those who embrace the faith. Many an innocent traveler has entered a temple of the Sect looking only for a night of pleasure in the festhall, and emerged a week later with new desires that no normal society could satisfy, or with new ambitions that could only be realized with the financial and political support of the Sect.

In short, the Sect seeks to make addicts of vice. Its free-flowing sensual pleasures encourage many people to come closer, thinking that they can enjoy a few sweet encounters but pull away from the precipice before it's too late. Some succeed — for a while. But eventually, the lure of pleasure and power draws the moths too close to the flames, and they burn.

The leader of the Deeptown temple, Carsten, is a consummate deceiver. He never betrays, since betrayal only makes enemies. Instead he seduces, offering that which the initiate most desires. Several times a year he sponsors the Festival of Plenty, an open celebration of indulgence that is widely attended by the faithful and the dubious alike, all drawn by the free flow of wine and revelry. The conventional wisdom around Deeptown is that the Sect isn't an evil cult in the sense of slaughter and conquest; its members are just decadent libertines, whose ample pleasures can be warily sampled and enjoyed. This is, of course, a short-sighted point of view, but one that Carsten gladly encourages even as he bows before the brimstone lords of Hell.

A map of the Sect's temple appears on the next page. It's a large rectangular structure centered around a raised platform and altar. The platform is flanked on four sides by banquet tables. The Sect serves food and drink around the clock, at reasonable prices. Minstrels provide entertainment, interrupted occasionally by brief greetings and lusty exhortations towards indulgence by acolytes at the altar. Four curtained festhall spaces provide private areas for parties and other, more intimate, forms of paid recreation. A stairwell in the east end leads to an upper floor thirty feet above, containing living space for the priest and acolytes as well as additional festhall space offering more unusual and expensive forms of pleasure.

Carsten

6th-Level Cleric

Hit Dice:	6d8+6 (39 hp)
Initiative:	+5 (+1 Dex, +4 Improved Initiative)
Speed:	20 ft.
AC:	18 (+5 Chainmail, +1 Dex, +2 Large Shield)
Attacks:	Longsword +6 melee
Damage:	Longsword 1d8+2
Face/Reach:	5 ft. by 5 ft./5 ft.
Special Qualities:	Normal cleric powers
Saves:	Fort +6, Ref +3, Will +8
Abilities:	Str 15, Dex 13, Con 12, Int 13, Wis 16, Cha 16
Skills:	Bluff +7, Concentration +3, Diplomacy +7, Gather Information +5, Hide -3 (incl. -7 armor penalty), Intimidate +4, Knowledge (Religion) +5, Scry +3, Spellcraft +3
Feats	Brew Poison, Heightened Spell, Improved Initiative, Maximize Spell
Challenge Rating:	6
Alignment:	Lawful Evil

Spells: Carsten typically prepares the following spells. He also has the 1st- through 4th-level domain spells for Evil and Trickery.
  0 Level: *detect magic, detect poison, guidance, inflict minor wounds, purify food and drink, read magic*
  1st Level: *curse water, divine favor, doom, inflict light wounds, obscuring mist*
  2nd Level: *darkness, death knell, hold person, undetectable alignment*
  3rd Level: *bestow curse, inflict serious wounds, summon monster III*
  4th Level: *divination*
  Evil Domain: *protection from good, desecrate magic circle against good, unholy blight*
  Trickery Domain: *change self, invisibility, nondetection, confusion*

The Temple of the Sect of Sixty

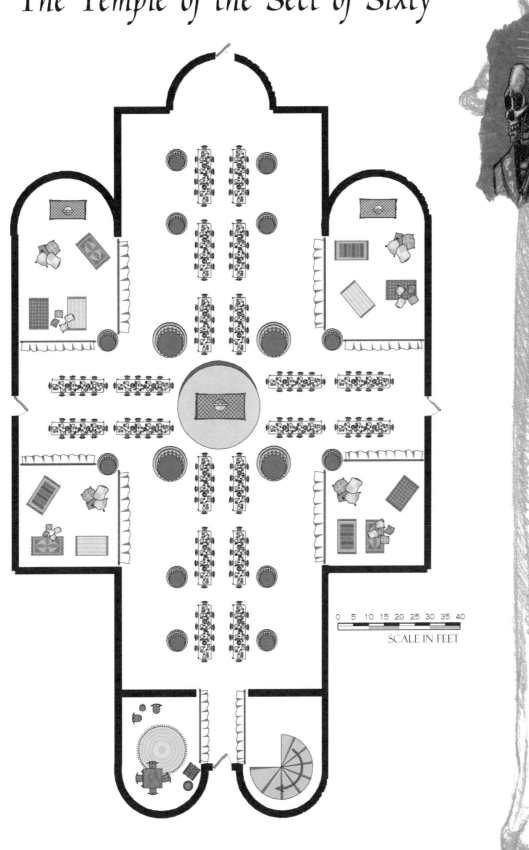

SCALE IN FEET

0 5 10 15 20 25 30 35 40

Upper
Forks

Deeptown

Forks Gate

Lower
Forks

Upper
Dream

Key

1 = Temple of the Holy Order

2 = Temple of the Sect of Sixty

3 = Deeptown City Hall

4 = Town Guard and Jail

5 = Inn of the White Horse

6 = Temple of All Hope

7 = House of Good Favor

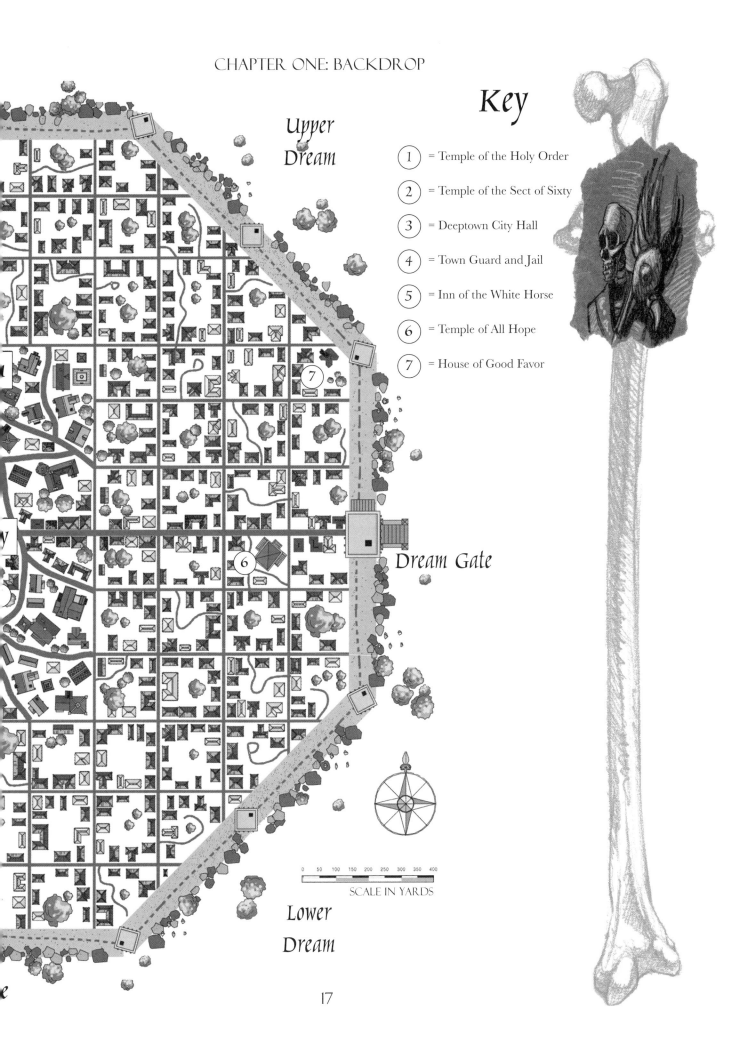

Dream Gate

0 50 100 150 200 250 300 350 400

SCALE IN YARDS

Lower

Dream

CHAPTER TWO

GETTING STARTED

For this scenario, the PCs need to be your basic muscle-for-hire. If this isn't the first scenario in your campaign, getting them to Deeptown is easy: hire them as caravan guards for a group of travelers that needs to get there. The travelers are coming for the Festival of Plenty, the Sect of Sixty's regular pageant of ribald debauchery. If you take this option, play out the caravan trip through the mountains and give the PCs a chance to learn about the Festival and Deeptown. At an opportune moment, stage an attack by a small bandit group of a half-dozen or so. This group isn't allied to Modus or Lucien; they're just one of the small bands operating briefly in the area.

Regardless of the situation, the PCs are in Deeptown in the midst of the Festival of Plenty, looking for work. Word on the street is good: pay rates for caravan guards leaving Deeptown are high, especially since the Festival is widely believed to attract unsavory people looking to separate fools from their money.

THE FESTIVAL OF PLENTY

This celebration lasts for three nights. The Sect of Sixty does not advertise its sponsorship, and indeed the temple building itself does not serve as a celebratory locale for the events; even so, its involvement in the Festival is widely known by word of mouth.

The Festival is held on the shores of Shadow Lake, just south of the town walls. Traveling merchants operate booths offering exotic goods, alongside Deeptown tavern owners who set up makeshift facilities in tents and pavilions. The Sect hires several dozen guards for the event, who all wear distinctive red sashes identifying them as keepers of the peace; the penalties for impersonating a guard are severe, usually involving a beating and subsequent placement in the Pit, one of the Festival's attractions.

The Pit is a twelve-foot deep by ten-feet square hole in the earth. The town council hands over an assortment of current criminal prisoners, who have their hands and ankles bound and are tossed into the Pit for a few hours on a rotating schedule. The crowd is welcome to hurl most anything down at the Pit's occupants so long as nothing like rocks or weapons are used; most commonly, the Pit serves as a latrine for the entire Festival. If criminals are in short supply, the Sect pays anyone desperate enough a handsome fee in exchange for incarceration in the Pit. (Some people even volunteer.) A few red-sashed guards stand nearby, ensuring that no one in the Pit is badly injured or drowns in the effluvia.

Other attractions are not so disgusting. The Sect provides tremendous quantities of wine and food at no charge, though it is careful to tailor its offerings so as not to duplicate the various merchants' specialized offerings. Several festhall tents are erected as well, for the pleasure of paying attendees.

At the heart of the Festival is a massive open space with music, dancing, and a few drunken fistfights. Each night, the Sect sets up a huge bonfire and the temple musicians form a drum circle to thump out an intoxicating, hypnotic rhythm. Crowds dance in rings around the fire, led in singing the traditional song of the Festival by well-placed Sect acolytes who look like ordinary revelers:

> *The wine, the song*
> *The dance, the fire*
> *Return, return, return*

On the last night, the Sect presents the *Passion of Arimbo,* a popular folk tale about a farmer who follows a jolly devil into the rings of Hell. There he experiences incredible pleasures, acted out on stage with great enthusiasm and copious nudity, only to be confronted by the prospect of losing his immortal soul. But the wily farmer bests the devil in a singing contest, and then leads the infernal horde on a merry, drunken dance that winds its way out into the crowds and around the bonfire again for an all-night party.

The true intent of this artful piece of propaganda should need no elaboration.

PCS AT THE FESTIVAL

The Festival of Plenty may be used in a couple of ways. If you want to get on with the scenario, you can just describe it briefly as something going on in the background, and then proceed directly to the next scene. Otherwise, by all means encourage the players to explore the Festival and enjoy it. They may take snickering delight in having their characters visit one of the festhalls for a roll in the hay, or settle down in one of the tavern tents to play a drinking game with other revelers. (Rules for a popular local drinking game appear in the boxed text on page 20.) Should the PCs visit the Festival, in fact, you should encourage this sort of behavior; rest assured that by the end of the scenario they'll get a taste of Hell that should make them look back at this event with a guilty conscience.

Another alternative for involving the PCs in the Festival of Plenty is to give them work as red-sashed guards. The Sect does the hiring for this gig through a friendly merchant named Salian, and it pays well. This provides opportunities for the PCs to get into a few non-fatal brawls with drunken revelers, and perhaps rescue someone in distress. Eventually they'll have the pleasure of seeing their detainees thrown into the Pit, and perhaps take the opportunity to laughingly relieve themselves. Again, encourage this sort of

ILLUSTRATION BY SCOTT REEVES

silly excess, since it'll set the rest of the events in stark relief.

If you want to have some fun with the Festival, here are some suggestions for encounters to offer the PCs:

- A drunken half-orc picks a fight with a PC elf or halfling. Should trouble start, he has some human friends who will either join in the non-lethal melee or pull their buddy back from serious danger.

- A red-sashed guard is getting beaten badly by some surly dwarves behind a tent. If the PCs intervene, the grateful guard gives them a token redeemable for an evening of enjoyment in a festhall tent operated by the Sect.

- An angry acolyte of the Holy Order storms through the crowd with a hand-lettered sign reading "No Pleasure Without Price!" He rants at anyone who will listen about the evils of the Sect of Sixty and how they're all fooling themselves about the nature of the Festival. Eventually some guards persuade him to leave.

- In a makeshift fighting ring, a tough dwarf (3rd-level fighter) will brawl with anyone (no weapons or armor) while his accomplice takes bets. Should someone get the better of the dwarf within five minutes, he or she wins a gold piece.

- A tavern tent catches fire during a bar fight. Nearby PCs are pressed into service for a bucket brigade from the lake, and are rewarded with free drinks when the crisis is over.

Drinking Game: I'll Kill You

"I'll Kill You" is a popular drinking game for two people that the PCs might get drawn into. While it is resolved with die rolls for gaming purposes, there is a roleplaying aspect to it as well that should be fun.

To play, the opponents sit across each other at a table with copious supplies of beer, wine, or other drinks. A third person serves as the judge; he or she must not be allied with either player, and is typically a random bar patron who gets free drinks from the players in return for this service.

The players take turns describing, in gleeful detail, exactly how they will kill each other, beginning with the words "I'll kill you . . ." They must take a sip of drink after every single word in their threat, and they must make the threats as entertaining and unusual as possible. After each player has made his or her threat and had the appropriate number of drinks, the judge decides the winner of that round, either by fiat or by acclamation of the crowd. A typical threat is something like "I'll kill you by ripping out your innards on the horns of a live goat!", which would require the speaker to take fifteen sips of drink. (The size of the sips varies widely and is not carefully monitored in most bars, although some have special little cups about the size of a thimble just for playing "I'll Kill You.") To win the game, you want to make the most entertaining threat in the fewest words possible. The winner of each round goes first the next round, allowing him to set the number of words for his opponent to play against. Play continues until one player passes out or gives up, which usually means buying a round for the bar, or until a fight breaks out.

In game terms, each round the two players must make an opposed 1d20 roll. They each get to add their Constitution bonus to the roll, as well as the number of words they used in their threat. In addition, and subject to the GM's discretion, they may add appropriate skill bonuses such as Bluff, Knowledge (Colorful Murder Techniques), or what have you. The highest adjusted result wins the round, unless the judge is dishonest.

When the round ends, however, take the lower number of drinks consumed and subtract it from the higher number. (If both players took the same number of sips, the result is 0.) The difference is then applied as a cumulative negative modifier to the higher-drinking player's roll in the next round and beyond. These modifiers keep adding up, meaning the wordier player soon becomes too impaired to win anymore. If either player's drunkenness modifier reaches their Constitution x 5, that player passes out and loses the whole game.

Example: Jarmik has a Con of 14 (modifier +2) and the skill Bluff with a modifier of +4, giving him a total modifier of +6. His opponent Claudius has a Con of 10 (modifier 0) and the skill Concentration with a modifier of +6, also giving him a total modifier of +6. In the first round, Jarmik says "I'll kill you with nothing but my ear!" (8 words) to which Claudius responds "I'll kill you with my sister's blood-rag and a handful of maggots!" (13 words). They roll an 8 and a 14, giving them adjusted totals of 22 (8 roll + 8 words + 6 modifier) for Jarmik and 33 (14 roll + 13 words + 6 modifier) for Claudius; Claudius wins the round handily. However, now Claudius has a drunkenness modifier of -6 (14 drinks - 8 drinks) for the next round and beyond; if he keeps using so many words, and drinking so heavily, he'll pass out and lose the game.

THE JOB

At some point after they arrive in Deeptown — possibly after an encounter at the Festival that proves their mettle — the PCs are approached by a sniveling little guy named Dorangus. He says he's got some "rough work" for them, and that his patron will pay handsomely for their time. For starters, he'll throw them a few silver coins just for coming to the meeting. If asked, he'll them that he does not know who wants to hire them; he's just a go-between.

The meeting is held that night at the House of Good Favor, a temple in Upper Dream whose priests were chased out a year ago for defrauding townsfolk in a pyramid scheme. (A map of the temple appears below.) It's been thoroughly looted and is frequently occupied by transients. The Trade Circle took possession of the land pending a new agreement with the church at some point in the future, and it doesn't care what happens to the building in the meantime — more damage now just means more construction contracts and permits later.

The temple is a modest one-story wooden structure. Many of the support beams have been hacked loose and reused by looters, resulting in the collapse of part of the roof a few months ago. The floor is now sodden with rain and the stench of those who sleep there. All of the furnishings are long gone, and the walls are defaced with graffiti.

Dorangus meets the PCs outside and leads them in. Inside are ten men wearing colorful animal masks purchased at the Festival, and all are armed with swords. They are standing around chatting about the Festival and looking casual. When Dorangus leads the PCs inside, they greet the party jovially. One of the men hands Dorangus a small sack of coins and he scurries away. Another offers the PCs a drink from a wineskin, but is not offended if they decline.

A third man steps forward and addresses the party. His exact words are up to the GM, but his message hits the following points:

- He does not give his name or identify himself in any useful way. He'll explain that this is for the PCs' protection as well as his own. (The man is actually Maxlus, Modus's lieutenant; Modus does not attend the meeting and in fact does not appear in this scenario if all goes well. The other men are Maxlus's squad. Note that Modus has given Maxlus his *ring*

The House of Good Favor

SCALE IN FEET

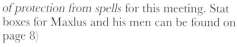

of protection from spells for this meeting. Stat boxes for Maxlus and his men can be found on page 8)

- There is a bandit lord named Lucien who operates in the eastern mountains, preying on caravans. The man gives the party a description of Lucien, saying he is about six feet tall with long red hair.

  - Lucien is making an alliance with an unknown group, which will increase his power.

  - The two groups are meeting in two days at a secret villa in the mountains to the north.

  - The party is to scout out the villa and make an assault.

  - The assault does not have to kill either group; the only goal is to disrupt the meeting and make Lucien look incompetent.

  - The party should hit them hard and then flee if they feel the battle is not going well. If Lucien is killed, their reward will be doubled — but his death is not required, and Lucien is a dangerous opponent.

  - The amount of the payment the man offers the PCs for the job is up to the GM. It should be substantial.

  - The man will buy them mundane equipment if they need it, such as horses, weapons, and armor. But half the cost of this equipment will come out of their final payment and this cost cannot be more than one-third of the total payment.

An Alternative

If you feel the PCs are unlikely to accept an assignment this mysterious and potentially questionable, there is an alternative. Cassius, the head priest of the Holy Order, can hire them for the same mission. He'll stress the importance of discretion, since he shouldn't be acting directly against the Sect, and explains that if questioned he will deny that this arrangement ever took place.

Ideally, however, you shouldn't use this option since it isn't nearly as interesting. But if you've got a party chock full of Paladins or paranoids, this is probably the way to go.

- The man provides some magical items to assist them. In particular, he gives them a *fireball wand* with one charge, to be saved for when they break off the assault.

- The man gives them a letter of deposit from the Temple of All Hope, which they can redeem no sooner than five days from now. The Temple guarantees the validity of the transaction, as they commonly do. This is how the party will receive payment. He encourages the PCs to check in with the Temple to verify the letter. (The Temple does so, although they do not know who made the deposit. The letter includes the names of the entire party, so that any survivors can easily claim the funds.)

- He expects Lucien to have about a half-dozen guards with him. He has no idea how many guards will be present from the other group, but believes it will not be very many.

- The party is to set off tomorrow afternoon. They should reach the villa the following evening, and should attack either that night or the next morning before the meeting ends.

The Magic Items

The masked man gives the PCs several minor magic items to assist them in the job. They are:

Wand of Fireballs: A thin wooden baton about the size of a ruler, with no distinguishing marks. It contains a 5th-level *fireball spell*, causing 5d6 damage to targets within a 20 ft. radius at a range of up to 520 ft. (DC13 for Reflex saving throw to halve damage.) The wand has one charge.

Orb of Sight: A black glass orb about the size of a billiard ball. Pressing the orb against your eye, you can see through it clearly. If you squeeze the orb, it provides low-light vision; this enables the user to see clearly at twice normal human distance even in low light. If you rotate the orb, it acts like a telescope, providing 1x to 4x magnification to your range of sight; the more you rotate it from its starting point, the greater the magnification. If you tap on the orb, it lets you see through all solid objects within half the current range of sight; walls and people alike become equally translucent. Taking the orb away from your eye turns off all the effects. A leather sling allows it to be strapped to your head and over one eye, which is useful for firing missile weapons since the effective missile range is reduced up to 4x.

Flare Pebbles: A bag of twenty pebbles. Each is enchanted with a cantrip. When thrown against a target, the pebble flares to a bright light on impact, causing the target to suffer a -1 penalty on attack rolls for 1 minute. (DC13 for Fortitude saving throw to negate.) They cause no damage, but up to three pebbles can be thrown at once at the same target. Pebbles cannot be reused.

Sleep Arrow: One enchanted arrow. Upon impact against any surface, roll 2d4; that many Hit Dice worth of targets within a 15 ft. radius of impact fall asleep for three minutes. (DC 13 for Will saving throw to negate.) Targets with lower Hit Dice are affected first; if not enough Hit Dice remain to affect the next target, those excess Hit Dice are ignored. The arrow cannot be reused.

If you believe that the PCs will need more help, give them an extra *sleep arrow* or two, or perhaps add another charge to the *wand of fireballs*. These magic items are intended to give the PCs a tactical advantage over their opponents, and to encourage strategic planning of the assault. Used wisely, these items can make a crucial difference in the climactic fight; they are not meant to be of much use in direct combat.

- Dorangus will meet them at the Inn of the White Horse tomorrow morning and accompany them while they make any purchases; all purchases are paid by letter of deposit from the temple, keeping the transactions anonymous. He will provide them with a map to the villa (see page 24) and send them on their way.

If the PCs are resistant to the offer, or demand more information, the man guardedly states that the Deeptown Trade Circle is concerned with Lucien's power, and that his potential alliance could well threaten the safety of many travelers along the trade route. He also says that the Trade Circle would certainly be grateful to anyone who could make the trade route safer. Note that none of this is a lie; if the PCs infer that the man therefore works for the Trade Circle, well — that's their assumption, isn't it? Maxlus is crafty and avoids lying if at all possible, since he doesn't want to be exposed as a liar and he doesn't want to get Modus in trouble by making promises or statements that can't be backed up. He says helpful and encouraging things without drawing direct connections, speaking cagily and leaving the PCs to fill in the blanks however they like.

If the PCs worked as caravan guards on their way to Deeptown, the man mentions this in passing: "Certainly we can all agree that bandits like Lucien prey on helpless caravans. Really, all I'm asking you to do is protect the caravans from bandits. You'll just be doing this offensively instead of defensively. Why not ambush them for a change?"

Ultimately, the PCs should agree. It's a scenario, after all, and if they're that stubborn you can always send them on a randomly-generated dungeon crawl.

(Should the PCs just flip out and attack, Maxlus and his men fight. Conveniently, Maxlus has bribed a handful of guardsmen to loiter nearby. If trouble erupts, he'll call for assistance and the guards will come running; either the PCs end up in the Festival Pit, escape this debacle and end the scenario, or the guardsmen kill them.)

SHOPPING WITH DORANGUS

The next morning brings the shopping trip. Dorangus meets them as promised at the Inn of the White Horse and accompanies them. The PCs can buy most any mundane equipment, and possibly some magic items as well if they have the budget. Dorangus acts impatient the entire time, eager to wrap this up and go collect his final payment from his patron.

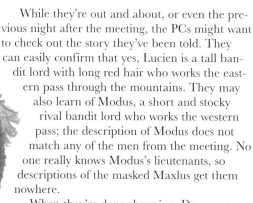

While they're out and about, or even the previous night after the meeting, the PCs might want to check out the story they've been told. They can easily confirm that yes, Lucien is a tall bandit lord with long red hair who works the eastern pass through the mountains. They may also learn of Modus, a short and stocky rival bandit lord who works the western pass; the description of Modus does not match any of the men from the meeting. No one really knows Modus's lieutenants, so descriptions of the masked Maxlus get them nowhere.

When they're done shopping, Dorangus leads them back to the inn and collects a map he left with the innkeeper. The map appears below, and may be photocopied for the players. He hands this to them, wishes them good luck, and splits.

If They Pull a Scam

Free-thinking PCs may decide to just take the equipment and magic items and bail on the whole assignment. They might even hang around a few days until the letter of deposit is redeemable and then attempt to collect it, as well.

Dorangus, who is your basic town scum, has instructions for this possibility. During the PCs' shopping trip, he's arranged for a number of other local scum to get a good look at the party. These men are indistinguishable from the other citizens and only swing by briefly before moving on, which shouldn't alert the PCs. If any of these men spot the party around town during the next couple of days, when they're supposed to be on the road, they'll alert Dorangus immediately. He'll pass the word to the innkeeper at the White Horse, who passes the word on to Maxlus. Maxlus pays some of Dorangus's pals to beat up the party while some others steal their horses, then Maxlus goes to the temple and withdraws the payment funds. He doesn't like people who break their promises.

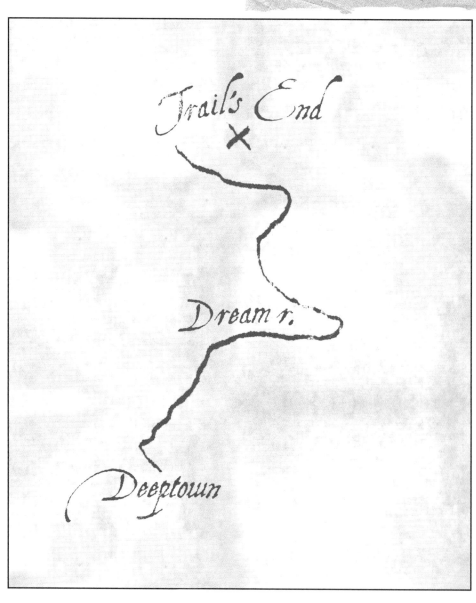

CHAPTER THREE

THE TREK NORTH

Map in hand, the party departs that afternoon. They'll be following the path of the Dream River as it winds its way up through the mountains. It's a slow uphill slog that rapidly tires the horses, but the trip is mostly uneventful. The PCs should be setting guards when they make camp and doing the other things that adventuring parties like to do when on the trail.

THE DEAD ACOLYTES

During the morning of the second day, the PCs find the scene of a battle. It's the remains of a small camp, complete with a still-smoldering campfire and some bedrolls. The bodies of two young men are here, slain by sword-blows. The men are wearing the robes of acolytes from the Holy Order. Their bodies have been stripped of valuables and weapons, and their ears have been cut off and taken, apparently after death.

Any PCs who have skills relating to local lore may get a roll to see if they recognize this situation. If successful, they remember that the orcs of the Hard Tribe to the north have a ritual of manhood that young orcs take when they're ready to claim their place as adults in the tribe: they venture out to collect the ears of non-orcs, and cannot return until they have a particular number. (Stories vary on the number of ears they must collect. It might be as few as six, or as many as sixty.)

If they search the camp, the PCs make a discovery: a small pouch lying in the grass, overlooked by the acolytes' assailants. It contains a small glass globe, inside of which is a yellowed, slitted eyeball floating in fluid. PCs with appropriate lore skills might recognize this eye as belonging to a devil or diabolical being of some sort.

The item is magical, and the eye always points to the nearest source of evil. Of course, the PCs may not realize this. What they soon realize, however, is that the eye continually points north, towards their destination; and indeed, when they reach the villa the eye points directly at it.

The players may well assume this is all a sign that Lucien is making a deal with the orcs. There they go, assuming things again …

TRAIL'S END

The villa, marked as Trail's End in the area map printed on the inside front cover, sits on a slim plateau on the side of a mountain. While there is a trail leading up to the villa, the structure is accessible on three sides through fairly mild

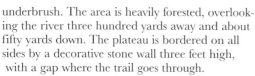

underbrush. The area is heavily forested, overlooking the river three hundred yards away and about fifty yards down. The plateau is bordered on all sides by a decorative stone wall three feet high, with a gap where the trail goes through.

Trail's End was built a decade ago by a merchant named Ivorus. He was captured by Lucien's men a couple years back during a caravan raid, and surrendered his goods and his villa to buy his freedom. Lucien uses it for recreational purposes, but considers it too exposed for use as a full-time headquarters.

The villa has two floors, as well as a large patio out front with an open fire pit. Floor plans for the villa appear on the inside back cover. Descriptions of the villa's rooms appear on pages 26 – 28.

Assuming the PCs have a lick of sense, they'll spend some time scoping out the plateau first. Using the *orb of seeing*, they can get a good look inside the villa as well.

THE ENEMY

Lucien is at the villa with nine guards, one of his assault squads; their stats appear on page 10. He's left the free squad with the other assault group, since the members of the free squad are better-trained and more intelligent; he doesn't want anyone with him who might have useful ambitions toward usurping his power by making a deal on the side with the Sect of Sixty.

As for the Sect, they've sent three acolytes along to make the deal; Carsten, the head priest, isn't about to risk his neck by venturing into the wilderness. Plus, he can always claim that his ambitious assistants tried to set up this deal without his knowledge, a plausible enough explanation given the nature of the Sect. Stats for the acolytes appear on page 13.

All told, then, there are thirteen people at the villa, three of whom have spells. The PCs are outnumbered, but they have the advantage of surprise, some magic of their own, and hopefully some good planning as to how they'll make the assault.

Six of Lucien's men are outside on watch at all times, using a rotating schedule. Their positions are marked on the inside cover map and they stick to those positions pretty well unless trouble erupts. Lucien remains inside with three of his men and the three acolytes. The group has fourteen horses, all of which are tethered behind the villa in the horse pen. Two men venture down to the river four times a day to retrieve buckets of water for the horses and the men. (The fourteenth horse is used by the acolytes of the Sect to transport the Bone Mirror, discussed later.)

Lucien and the acolytes spend their time drinking and talking. If the PCs do nothing, then the negotiations go well and a deal is struck.

Both groups go to sleep after dark. The guards sleep and watch in shifts, always keeping six men awake and reasonably alert; the three men off

duty sleep in the servants' quarters. At night the guards on duty keep a small fire stoked in the patio fire pit, with ample wood at hand to raise the flames if they need light, as well as torches and lanterns. By night, Lucien sleeps in the master bedroom and the acolytes sleep in the easternmost bedroom, all on the upper floor.

The PCs have the cover of the forest from which to make their lookout, and can easily scale the taller trees for a clear view of the villa. It shouldn't take them long to size up the situation and hatch a plan.

THE VILLA

Trail's End is a two-story villa with high, peaked roofs and numerous windows and doors. In general, this is a very well-furnished house; however, a couple years of occasional visits by Lucien and his crew have left it a bit rough around the edges.

All windows to the house are glass-paned, swing open on hinges, and offer little security. They can easily be smashed and entered. Likewise, the doors lock but provide only DC 12 resistance. (When the original owner had this place, he left a couple of servants and guards here at all times.) All rooms include little shelves to hold candles or lanterns, as needed. There are no overhead light fixtures such as chandeliers.

Descriptions of the villa's rooms follow.

GROUND FLOOR

Common Room: This very large space provides a congenial assembly area with chairs and a fireplace, as well as numerous windows looking onto the back patio. Two dozen candles rest along the fireplace mantel. A staircase next to the front door leads to the upper floor, while a door in the southeast corner opens onto the front patio. The ceiling above the northwest section of the room is twice as high as the rest of the ground floor, reaching up through the upper floor to the roof. A balcony on the second floor facing the back patio looks down on the fireplace and carpet.

Library: West of the common room and just south of the octagonal hall, the library is a cozy room ringed with shelves. The former owner's collection of religious and historical manuscripts would be worth 500 gp to buyers in Deeptown, though it would require a wagon or several horses to transport and is not obviously valuable. In addition to the books, the shelves are littered with assorted curios, including a goblin skull, the mounted head of a minotaur, assorted fine glassware, and other odds and ends. The large table contains two oil-filled lanterns, which Lucien's crew does not use.

Storage Rooms: These two closets contain mundane supplies for the former household, such as extra linens, candles, lantern oil, and cleaning supplies.

Servants' Quarters: The owner of the villa used this room to house the small band of servants and guards who staffed the villa. A door in the east wall opens onto the back patio. A small fireplace stands in the southeast corner, sharing a chimney with the master fireplace. The table at the north wall holds an oil lantern. At night, Lucien's guards bed down here when they aren't on duty. They leave the lantern lit but hooded, ready to flood the room with light in case of trouble.

Kitchen: This open area to the east of the common room includes a large water basin, cupboards, and a variety of pots, pans, and culinary tools. In addition, there is a substantial quantity of spices and herbs. There is no stove, however, as cooking is performed in the front patio firepit. Instead, this is where food is prepared for cooking and then for serving. The table to the southeast holds an oil lantern.

Dining Room: Here sits a handsome long table with seating for ten, open to the kitchen. A door in the west wall leads to the back patio.

Courtyard Patio: This large tiled patio has a sizable fire pit in the center ringed with blackened flagstones. Two short posts flank the fire pit, allowing a large spit to be laid across it for roasting carcasses. Lucien's men keep a small fire stoked in the pit by night.

Back Patio: Another tiled patio, this one with four massive columns that support the overhanging rear roof. Lucien's horses are tethered in the trees just north of this patio.

UPPER FLOOR

Landing: The staircase from the common room opens into this generous space on the upper floor, featuring a balcony that overlooks the floor below. The balcony has a wooden railing four feet high, DC 16 to smash through in case someone feels like throwing an enemy against it; tossing him or her over the side is much easier and results in a 15 ft. fall.

Parlor: A rather elegant chamber with a piano, the parlor is perhaps the least-used room in the house now that Lucien and his thugs own the place.

Eastern Bedrooms: These two bedrooms are both attractive places that have seen little of Lucien's hard use. Typically, he stays in the master bedroom and makes his men sleep on the ground floor. The acolytes from the Sect of Sixty are staying in the larger of the two bedrooms. Both rooms have oil lanterns on the desks as well as candle shelves.

Lounge: Another room that sees little use by Lucien, though he occasionally retires here with one of his would-be lieutenants for late-night drinks and games of mumblety-peg. A candelabra stand rests atop the table.

Master Bedroom: Lucien gives this room plenty of use, and it shows. The place smells dank, the sheets haven't been changed in two years, and the carpet is covered in dubious stains. Candles rest atop the fireplace mantle, and oil lanterns sit atop both desks. The floor is typically strewn with dirty clothes and the remains of unfinished meals.

PLANNING STRATEGY

At this point, we've arrived at the heart of the scenario. The design goal of "Three Days To Kill" is to simulate a Tom Clancy-style Special Ops mission, but in a sword and sorcery setting. The magic items provided to the PCs are fantasy analogues of modern technological gear: the *orb of seeing* serves as binoculars and nightvision goggles (plus x-ray gogs!), the *sleep arrows* are knockout gas, the *flare pebbles* are flash grenades, and the *fireball wand* is a rocket launcher.

The players *must* study the villa, figure out how many targets there are, and make an effective plan to hit the place. If they just charge the front door, they'll almost certainly get slaughtered. The magic items are intended as a slap upside the head to encourage them to think strategically. In case they need some help, or want to make some skill checks to get ideas of what to do, here's a suggested strategy for taking the villa by night:

- Someone climbs a tree to use the *orb of seeing* to sketch a floor plan of the villa, and the position of everyone inside and out. He or she should recognize Lucien from the description provided by their employer.
- Put one archer in a tree close to the villa's eastern side.
- Station half the party (team A) on the western slope close to the servants' quarters, but below the wall.
- Station the other half of the party (team B) on the western slope just in front of the villa, but below the wall.
- The archer pops the guard on the patio with a normal arrow, probably not fatally; the archer could use a blunted arrow to ensure the target lives. The guard yells for help.
- Other guards come running through the dark to the firepit where the injured man is. The archer lobs a *sleep arrow* onto the patio in their midst.
- Team A rushes the servants' quarters through the rear windows, slaughtering the three unarmed and sleeping bandits in the room before they know what's going on; they use the *flare pebbles* if needed.
- Team B comes over the low wall into the courtyard and kills the guards outside, most of

whom are hopefully asleep. Any guards still awake out here get shot in the back by the archer as they cross the front yard to engage Team B on the western side.
- Teams A and B rendezvous in the common room at the base of the stairs and head up.
- Team A goes after Lucien, while Team B goes for the three strangers sleeping in the easternmost bedroom.
- If things go badly upstairs, both teams retreat to the front yard. The archer provides cover while the wand-carrier lets loose a *fireball* through the front door at any pursuers.
- Run away.

This plan is reasonably sound, and it only relies on the magic items provided for the job; the party's own magical abilities will also come into play and allow for even better strategies.

Of course, no plan can anticipate the unexpected …

THE BONE MIRROR

When the assault begins, the three acolytes flee to the easternmost bedroom on the upper floor while Lucien marshals his troops to repel the attack. (If the attack is by night, the acolytes are probably already there asleep.) The villa is not easily defensible, however, owing to its many windows and six entrances.

As the battle gets underway, the acolytes get busy. They've brought along a magic artifact intended as a demonstration for Lucien of their supernatural powers. The artifact is called the Bone Mirror, and it spells trouble.

The Bone Mirror is a portal to Hell. It's about six feet tall and four feet wide, made of a dark glassy substance and bordered by aged human bones bound together with tendons. One of the acolytes steps through it at the first opportunity to recruit assistance from their diabolical allies. (To pass through the Bone Mirror, you must be wearing a medallion of the Sect; without it, it's just a bad mirror.)

What does the acolyte bring back with him? That's up to the GM to decide. Several creatures are described below; you can use some of them, multiples of them, or whatever you like. This little twist is here so you can make the combat tougher if the PCs are doing too well, and also to give them a nasty surprise.

The bandits really weren't expecting monsters to start showing up. Although the creatures are initially going after the PCs, it won't take long for some freaked-out bandit thug to take a swing at one of them. Once that happens, the combat turns into a free-for-all, with the minions of Hell out for everyone's blood.

FROM HELL

The monsters from the Bone Mirror available to the acolytes include Black Dogs, Wicker Men, and Leprous Striders, among others.

Beasts continue emerging from the Bone Mirror as often or as rarely as the GM wants, even if the acolytes are killed. The only way to stop their coming through is to smash the Bone Mirror, which is easily done — if you can reach it. (If none of the PCs are clever enough to smash the mirror, have one of the bandits do it; these guys are pretty freaked out by the sight of the creatures.)

Of course, smashing the Bone Mirror only makes things worse.

THE BONE CHURCH

Smashing the Bone Mirror stops any more diabolical creatures from emerging. As the mirror shatters, PCs nearby get a brief glimpse through its flying shards of what lies beyond: Hell itself. They only get flashing, fractured images of fire and stone and screaming souls, and then the glass and bones fall to the floor.

A few moments later, however, all the pieces of the Bone Mirror start bleeding. If any of the PCs have the eye-globe from the dead acolytes, it shatters messily.

The blood wells up from the broken edges of the mirror and oozes out of the bones. For the first three rounds, it's just a few trickles. Then blood comes faster, coating the floor around the

shards, and begins to expand rapidly. Tendrils shoot out across the floor and begin running up the walls. As the blood spreads, it transforms the surfaces of the room. The floor bulges, and bones, flesh, and faces begin to form under the PCs' feet. The effect spreads rapidly, accompanied by the screams of the damned. Within five minutes, the entire villa is transformed into an outpost of Hell; a pulsing, living, screaming conglomeration of bodies. If any of the acolytes or creatures are still alive during this process, they begin screaming joyously about "the coming of He Who Walks!" Any bandits still alive soon flee the house. The PCs will probably do the same.

THE ORCS

In case the players were wondering about those ear-happy orcs, well — wonder no more. Six young orcs from the Hard Tribe have been scoping out the villa themselves, hungry to prove their manhood. They had decided against attacking it just yet, hoping instead to pick off a few of the inhabitants when they got back on the trail to go home. Watching the chaos of the assault, however, they've decided it's the perfect opportunity.

As people begin fleeing the house from the onrush of Hell, the orcs charge up the slopes and start killing anyone convenient. They're not very experienced fighters, but under the circumstances they've got a shot at getting in a few good whacks.

ILLUSTRATION BY DAVID WHITE

Wicker Man, Medium

Smoldering Wrath

Hit Dice:	2d10+6 (14 hp)
Initiative:	+1 (Dex)
Speed:	10 ft.
AC:	15 (+1 Dex, +4 Natural)
Attacks:	Scythe +4 melee
Damage:	Scythe 2d4+3 + poison
Face/Reach:	5 ft. by 5 ft./5 ft.
Special Attacks:	Poison, Death Explosion
Special Qualities:	Darkvision 60 ft., Degrades
Saves:	Fort +3, Ref +1, Will +0
Abilities:	Str 16, Dex 12, Con 16, Int 10, Wis 10, Cha 6
Skills:	Jump +3, Spot +1
Feats:	Weapon Focus (Scythe)
Climate/Terrain:	Hell, or elsewhere when summoned
Organization:	Solitary
Challenge Rating:	2
Alignment:	Lawful Evil

A Wicker Man is the hollow shell of a humanoid figure, woven from thorny vines and completely filled with smoldering brimstones. Its eyes are burning coals. Denizens of Hell, Wicker Men rarely appear in our world because they cannot last very long away from their natural plane. Most Wicker Men wield scythes of black rock that ooze a poisonous ichor.

Poison (Ex): When damaged by the scythe, the PC suffers a -4 attack penalty for three minutes. (Make a Fortitude saving throw to negate; DC is 10 + HP damage done in the attack.)

Death Explosion (Su): When a Wicker Man is reduced to 0 HP or less, it explodes in a blast of brimstone. This explosion causes 1d6 damage to everyone within 15 ft. (Make a DC 13 Reflex saving throw to negate.)

Darkvision (Ex): A Wicker Man may see even without any light whatsoever, to a range of 60 ft.

Degrades (Su): Each minute it spends in our world, a Wicker Man suffers 1d3 damage from its own burning brimstone core.

DEPARTURE

Although the acolytes' boasting about the coming of He Who Walks comes to nothing — for now — it's unlikely that the PCs and bandits stick around to find this out. Surviving bandits get to their horses if possible, and then take off into the mountains. Remaining acolytes and creatures stay in the new Bone Church, doing unsavory things with the corpses at hand. The PCs should just get the Hell out.

Behind them, the Bone Church crouches on the side of the mountain, pulsing and screaming into the night.

Black Dog, Medium

Howling Fetch of the Inferno

Hit Dice:	1d8+2 (7 hp)
Initiative:	+7 (+3 Dex, +4 Improved Initiative)
Speed:	40 ft.
AC:	15 (+3 Dex, +2 Natural)
Attacks:	Bite +1 melee
Damage:	Bite 1d6+1
Face/Reach:	5 ft. by 5 ft./5 ft.
Special Attacks:	Howl
Special Qualities:	Darkvision 60 ft.
Saves:	Fort +2, Ref +3, Will +0
Abilities:	Str 12, Dex 16, Con 14, Int 6, Wis 10, Cha 6
Skills:	Listen +2, Move Silently +5, Spot +2
Feats:	Improved Initiative
Climate/Terrain:	Hell, or elsewhere when summoned
Organization:	Native in packs, usually solitary when summoned
Challenge Rating:	1
Alignment:	Lawful Evil

A Black Dog is a large black mastiff who is often dispatched from Hell to serve those loyal to the infernal realms. Under ordinary circumstances, a Black Dog looks like a normal dog, if an unfriendly one. During combat, however, a Black Dog's eyes glow a fiery magical red.

Darkvision (Ex): A Black Dog may see even without any light whatsoever, to a range of 60 ft.

Howl (Su): Once per day a Black Dog may use its Howl attack. Howl causes all non-lawful evil targets within a 20 ft. radius to make a Will saving throw or suffer a -2 attack penalty for 1 minute. Targets must be able to hear a Black Dog's mournful cry to be affected.

Toughening the Enemy

If you believe your PCs need more of a challenge than what's provided, there are a few options you can take. First, Lucien can bring the free squad instead of the assault squad, providing bandits with better fighting skill but fewer numbers. Second, he can bring both an assault squad and the free squad; in this case, the free squad stays on duty outside the entire time to keep them away from the Sect representatives. Third, you can send Carsten along with his acolytes, though he poses a real threat to the PCs. Fourth, you can add more orcs to the final encounter. And finally, you can always send more monsters through the Bone Mirror.

Leprous Strider, Large

Minion of Hell

Hit Dice:	3d8+9 (22 hp)
Initiative:	+7 (+3 Dex, +4 Improved Initiative)
Speed:	40 ft.
AC:	19 (+3 Dex, +6 Natural)
Attacks:	Bite +4 melee, or 4 Claws +4 melee
Damage:	Bite 1d8+4, 4 Claws 1d6+2
Face/Reach:	5 ft. by 5 ft./5 ft.
Special Attacks:	Breath Weapon
Special Qualities:	Darkvision 60 ft.
Saves:	Fort +3, Ref +3, Will +0
Abilities:	Str 18, Dex 16, Con 16, Int 10, Wis 10, Cha 6
Skills:	Climb +6, Jump +8
Feats:	Improved Initiative
Climate/Terrain:	Hell, or elsewhere when summoned
Organization:	Solitary
Challenge Rating:	3
Alignment:	Lawful Evil

A Leprous Strider is a tall, gangly beast that stands 8 ft. high on six stilt-like legs. Its humanoid torso is covered in diseased, oozing flesh resembling the effects of leprosy. A Leprous Strider has the face of a human child, with blank white eyes and pudgy, drooling lips.

Breath Weapon (Su): Once per minute, a Leprous Strider may spew acid in a cone 15 ft. long, and up to 10 ft. wide. Targets in the cone take 1d8+2 damage. (DC 13 Reflex saving throw to negate.) Equipment struck must also save or take a -2 penalty to future use.

Darkvision (Ex): A Leprous Strider may see even without any light whatsoever, to a range of 60 ft.

Aftermath

Unless the PCs were decisively defeated, the alliance between Lucien and the Sect of Sixty breaks down before it starts. Lucien, if he survives, swears off diabolism for good and goes back to work. Modus doesn't confront him over the issue and the two continue their uneasy alliance. If Lucien didn't survive, his men scatter and Modus soon expands his operations to encompass the entire valley.

Six Young Orcs of the Hard Tribe

Boys Being Boys

Hit Dice:	1d8 (8, 6, 4, 4, 4, 3 hp)
Initiative:	+1 (Dex)
Speed:	20 ft.
AC:	+4 (+1 Dex, +3 Hide)
Attacks:	Warhammer +2 melee, or Dagger +2 melee
Damage:	Warhammer 1d8+2, Dagger 1d4+2
Face/Reach:	5 ft. by 5 ft./5 ft.
Special Qualities:	Sensitive to Sunlight
Saves:	Fort +0, Ref +1, Will +1
Abilities:	Str 14, Dex 12, Con 11, Int 10, Wis 9, Cha 8
Skills:	Listen +4, Spot +3
Feats:	Alertness
Climate/Terrain:	The foothills north of the Deeps
Organization:	Gang/Tribe
Challenge Rating:	1/2
Alignment:	Chaotic Evil

Sensitive to Sunlight: In the bright light of day or within magical light, orcs suffer a -1 penalty to their attack rolls.

The Sect's leader Carsten considers the whole thing a mess. If he gets word of the Bone Church, he'll send a few acolytes up to check it out — but it really isn't something he's very happy about, since the appearance of an infernal outpost in the heart of the Deeps is going to get him in trouble with the rival Holy Order and the Trade Circle. Being a clever minion of Hell, he'll probably go straight to the Trade Circle and inform them of this strange incursion of manifest evil, which he claims to have nothing to do with. He'll urge that a cabal of good-aligned priests go up there and shut the thing down, probably by lobbing barrels of holy water at it until it melts into goo. Of course, such a cabal needs some stalwart muscle-for-hire to accompany them on the trip — like the PCs, for example.

Even with this cunning plan, Carsten may be in trouble. Should the PCs go to the Trade Circle or the Holy Order and spill the beans, they'll be thanked for their efforts and probably hired to accompany the cabal. If this is the case, Carsten is promptly executed and the Sect of Sixty temple burned to the ground — at least until the Sect strikes a new deal with the Trade Circle.

After all, everyone loves the Festival of Plenty.

Future Adventures

First and foremost, of course, there is the matter of the Bone Church. As described, the PCs could easily end up hired to either travel there with a cabal of clerics, or they could get in on the sacking of the Sect's temple. The acolytes' raving about the coming of He Who Walks suggests that something unpleasant may appear in the Bone Church at some point, a possibility that should be headed off before it is realized.

Independent of this, there are other opportunities. However things work out, Modus is probably quite pleased with the outcome. He might offer the PCs the option of joining his Raiders; this wouldn't really be a good thing to do, of course, but the PCs might be suborned by the Trade Circle into infiltrating the Raiders and assisting in an attack to end Modus's operations for good.

In addition, the Holy Order may end up being the PCs' new friends. If the Sect's temple in Deeptown gets the sack, the Order is liable to take this opportunity to smash Sect temples in the towns on either side of the valley as well. Hiring the PCs to lead these operations would help the Order keep its hands clean.

And finally, the Sect of Sixty is likely to be out for some revenge. Ignorant of Modus's involvement, they'll target the PCs as Holy Order catspaws. Since Dorangus and half the scum in Deeptown have gotten a good look at the party, they'll be ready to sell the PCs out for thirty pieces of silver at the first opportunity.

Challenge Ratings

Here are the Challenge Ratings for all the likely opponents in the adventure. While the combined CR of even just the default opponents is substantial, there are three mitigating factors in the party's favor. The first is strategy: wise use of the magic items provided by Maxlus, as well as the party's own abilities, can make short work of the assault squad. The second is inter-group melee: shortly after the diabolic creatures begin emerging, surviving and panicked bandits begin fighting them; when the orcs show up, they fight everybody. This means that the PCs will not be alone against all these forces. The final factor is their mission: their goal is to disrupt the meeting, not to slaughter everyone; there's no reason to stick around once they've made a good hit, so let loose that *fireball wand* and run away!

Default Opponents

Lucien	4
Assault Squad	4.5 (1/2 x 9)
Acolytes	3
Black Dog	1
Wicker Man	2
Leprous Strider	3
Orcs	3 (1/2 x 6)

Optional Opponents

Free Squad	5 (1 x 5)
Carsten	6

Open Game License (Simplified)
Version .03